D1105407

WEIRD-BUT-TRUE FACTS ABOUT SPORTS

BY ARNOLD RINGSTAD | ILLUSTRATED BY KATHLEEN PETELINSEK

Published by The Child's World®
1980 Lookout Drive • Mankato, MN 56003-1705
800-599-READ • www.childsworld.com

Acknowledgments
The Child's World®: Mary Berendes, Publishing Director
Red Line Editorial: Editorial direction
The Design Lab: Design
Amnet: Production

ISBN 9781614734185
LCCN 2012946525

Printed in the United States of America
Mankato, MN
November, 2012
PA02143

About the Author

Arnold Ringstad lives in Minneapolis,
Minnesota. He wants to go golfing on
the moon.

About the Illustrator

Kathleen Petelinsek loves to draw and
paint. She lives next to a lake in southern
Minnesota with her husband, Dale; two
daughters, Leah and Anna; two dogs,
Gary and Rex; and her fluffy cat, Emma.

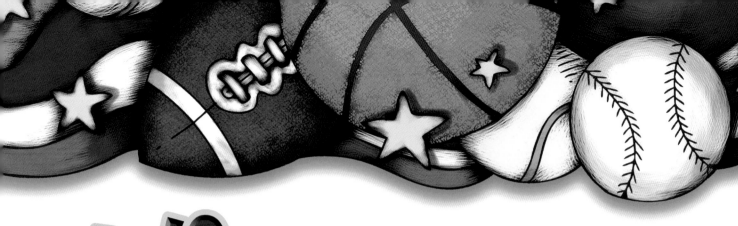

TABLE OF CONTENTS

INTRODUCTION

From unicycles to lunar golf, the world of sports is never dull. Many weird sports are played in the United States and around the world. If you can throw it, kick it, or race against it, it has probably been part of a sporting event. Get ready to learn about the weird world of sports—and remember, these facts are all true!

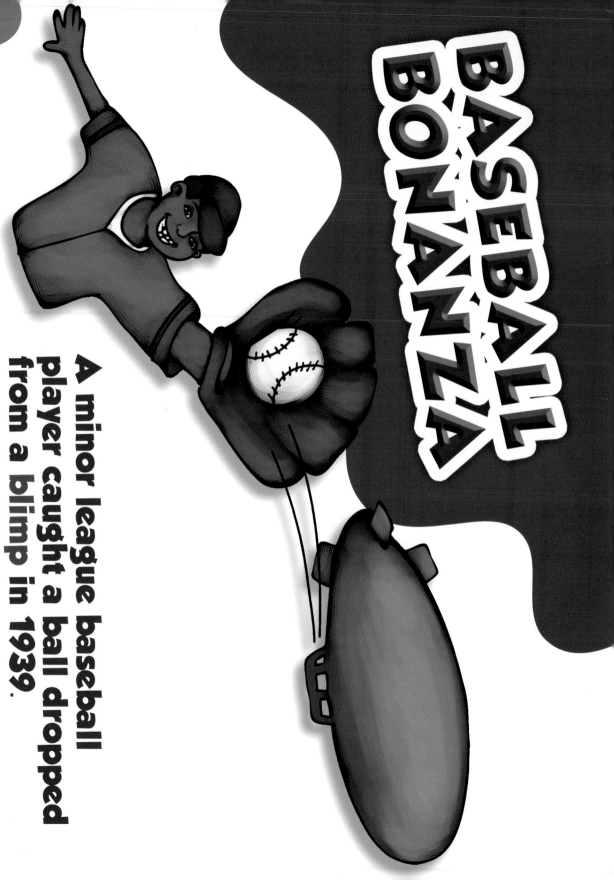

BASEBALL BONANZA

A minor league baseball player caught a ball dropped from a blimp in 1939.

The ball was dropped from 1,500 feet (450 m). The ball's speed caused the player's glove to smack into his face, giving him cuts and knocking out five teeth.

A baseball travels further through the air when it is hot and humid than when it is cold and dry.

This is because high temperatures and humidity make the air less dense.

This decreases air resistance, making the ball go further.

Baseball player Dave Winfield was drafted for three sports in 1973.

Teams in Major League Baseball (MLB), the National Basketball Association (NBA), and the National Football League (NFL) all wanted him.

Pitcher Randy Johnson accidentally killed a bird with a pitch in 2001.

Before 1859, baseball umpires sat in chairs behind home plate instead of crouching.

When Mark McGuire hit 70 home runs in 1998, they traveled a total of almost 30,000 feet (9,150 m).

Early baseball players used their bare hands to catch the ball.

They started using gloves in the 1870s.

In 1903, players earned approximately $1,200 as a bonus for winning the World Series.

By 2011, that amount had risen to more than $300,000 apiece.

BASKETBALL BASICS

The first basketballs were brown in color.

They were changed to orange in the 1950s to make it easier for players and fans to see them.

Basketball on horseback was popular for a brief time in the 1920s.

The game featured no **dribbling** and had fewer points than regular basketball.

James Naismith invented basketball to keep students busy indoors during the cold winter months.

The first basketball players used peach baskets instead of hoops with nets.

Play had to stop after each basket so a **referee** could climb a ladder and get the ball back.

An NBA basketball is designed to last for 50,000 bounces.

Slamball is a version of basketball played with four large **trampolines** in front of each net.

Players use the trampolines to spin and somersault in the air as they dunk the ball.

In 1974, a 13-year-old Swedish basketball player scored 272 points in a single game.

His team won the game 272-0.

Gheorghe Muresan was the tallest player in NBA history, standing 7 feet, 7 inches (2.3 m).

The Romanian played in the NBA from 1993 to 2000.

Tyrone Curtis "Muggsy" Bogues was the shortest player in NBA history, standing 5 feet, 3 inches (1.6 m).

He played in the NBA from 1987 to 2001, mostly for the Charlotte Hornets. He played for a time with Manute Bol, who at 7 feet, 6 inches (2.3 m) was one of the tallest players ever.

Slam dunks were banned in college basketball from 1967 to 1976.

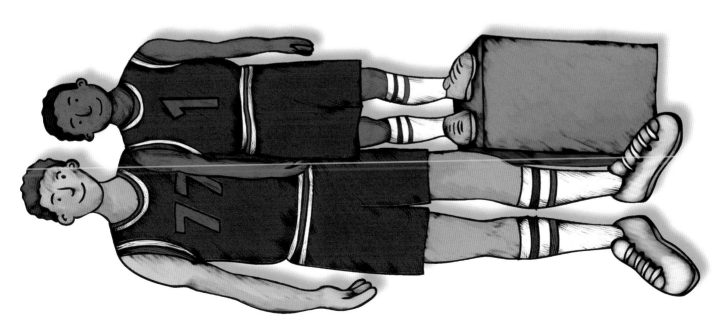

FOOTBALL FUN

The lowest ticket price for Super Bowl I, played in 1967, was $6.

The lowest ticket price for Super Bowl XLV, played in 2011, was $600.

Each year, the NFL uses 12,046 footballs.

It takes leather from approximately 1,200 cows to make them all.

In 1916, Georgia Tech won a college football game against Cumberland 222–0.

It is considered the worst loss ever in college football.

A player was paid $10 to play in a football game in 1895.

John Brallier is considered the first professional football player. In 2011, the highest-paid player was Peyton Manning, who made $23 million.

For each NFL game, the home team must provide 24 footballs.

The referees check the air pressure of each ball before the game.

The name of every NFL team ends in the letter "s."

In 2007, football player Chad Johnson raced on foot against a horse for charity— and he won.

Eli Manning and Peyton Manning are the only set of brothers to both play **quarterback** and play against each other in a **Super Bowl**.

Both have won the Most Valuable Player award.

TENNIS TRIVIA

The fastest recorded tennis serve went 163.4 miles per hour (263 km/h).

It was served by Australian player Samuel Groth in 2012.

About 42,000 tennis balls are used during the Wimbledon Championship.

Tennis player Roger Federer was the number one tennis player in the world for a record 237 straight weeks.

The previous record was 160 weeks, set by Jimmy Connors.

The longest tennis match in history was 11 hours and five minutes.

It was spread over three days of play in 2010.

WEIRD SPORTS

In chess boxing, players switch back and forth between playing chess and boxing.

They can win by either checkmate or knockout.

British divers created underwater hockey in 1954.

They invented it so they could stay in shape when it was too cold to dive outdoors. The sport is played in an indoor pool and is called Octopush in the United Kingdom.

The 1900 Olympics in Paris included a pigeon-shooting event.

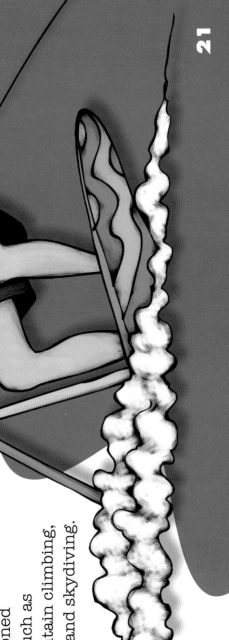

In extreme ironing, people iron their clothes in strange places.

Competitors have ironed while doing things such as snowboarding, mountain climbing, diving, waterskiing, and skydiving.

Pumpkin boat racing is a popular autumn sport.

People hollow out giant pumpkins, turn them into boats, and race them around a lake. Some of the biggest events take place in Maine, Oregon, Wisconsin, and Germany.

A 22-mile (35 km) race between people and horses is held in Wales.

It has been held each year since 1980. A person didn't win the race until 2004.

In cheese rolling, a large wheel of cheese is rolled down a hill, and people chase after it.

They usually don't catch it, since it quickly reaches speeds of 70 miles per hour (110 km/h).

There are 53 registered unicycle hockey teams in Germany.

MORE AMAZING FACTS ABOUT SPORTS

A hockey fan threw a live chicken onto the ice in a 1988 game.

Craig Rodenfels, a fan of the Los Angeles Kings, was thrown out of the game and arrested. He was charged with animal cruelty. Police said he was not arrested before throwing the chicken because it's not illegal to carry around a chicken.

The world's largest stadium can hold more than 250,000 people.

It is the Indianapolis Motor Speedway.

Boxer George Foreman named all five of his sons George.

The sports teams of the University of California, Santa Cruz, are called the Banana Slugs.

A student poll changed the name to the Sea Lions in 1980, but the new name did not stick. A new vote in 1986 reinstated the Banana Slugs. The mascot symbolizes the university's belief that athletics are important for all students, not just star athletes.

In the closest finish in NASCAR history, two drivers finished a race only .002 seconds apart.

It was a 2003 race at Darlington Raceway in South Carolina.

Only two days of the year have no major professional sports games.

They are the day before and the day after the MLB All-Star Game.

The first sport to be filmed was boxing.

Thomas Edison filmed a boxing match in 1894.

LOST GOLF BALL

Approximately 300 million golf balls are lost or thrown away in the United States each year.

In bowling, hitting three strikes in a row is called a "turkey."

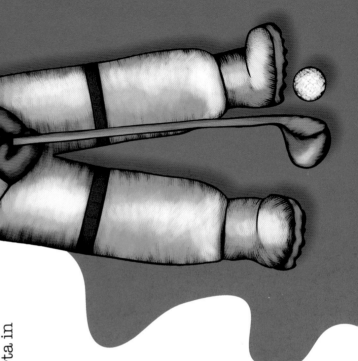

Astronauts have played golf on the moon.

In 1971, astronaut Alan Shepard hit two golf balls on the moon's surface. In addition, fellow astronaut Edgar Mitchell threw an improvised javelin.

The world's largest dodgeball game included 4,979 people.

It was played at the University of Alberta, in February 2012.

Tenpin bowling was invented to get around gambling laws.

Ninepin bowling was banned in the 1840s after people used it to gamble. The law didn't ban bowling completely, so players added a tenth pin to the game.

GLOSSARY

blimp (BLIMP)
A huge balloon that can carry people from place to place. Dropping baseballs from a blimp can be dangerous.

charity (CHAYR-it-ee)
A group of people that collects money for people in need. An athlete often helps a charity.

drafted (DRAFT-id)
Chosen to play on a team. Dave Winfield was drafted in three sports.

dribbling (DRIB-bull-ing)
Bouncing the ball in a basketball game. Dribbling a basketball many times can wear it out.

quarterback (KWOR-ter-back)
The football player who gets the ball at the beginning of a play. Peyton Manning is a quarterback.

referees (ref-er-EES)
The people at a sports game who make sure the rules are followed. Referees check the footballs before a game.

trampolines (tram-poh-LEENS)
Pieces of canvas stretched across frames that you can use to jump higher. Slamball is a kind of basketball that uses trampolines.

LEARN MORE

BOOKS

Belsky, Gary and Neil Fine.
*23 Ways to Get to First Base:
The ESPN Uncyclopedia.*
Bristol, CT: ESPN, 2007.

Wulf, Steve. *ESPN: The
Mighty Book of Sports
Knowledge.* Bristol, CT:
ESPN, 2009.

WEB SITES

Visit our Web site for links
about weird sports facts:
childsworld.com/links

*Note to Parents, Teachers, and
Librarians: We routinely verify our
Web links to make sure they are safe
and active sites. So encourage your
readers to check them out!*

INDEX